SPIRIT COOKING WITH YAEL

Recipes & Bible Meditations from the Holy Land

WINTERS
PUBLISHING GROUP

YAEL ECKSTEIN

Published by Winters Publishing
2448 E. 81st St.
Suite #4802
Tulsa, OK 74137

Book design copyright © 2014 by Winters Publishing. All rights reserved.
Cover and Interior Design by Stephanie Mora
Illustrations by Katie Brooks

Published in the United States of America

ISBN: 978-1-63185-587-0
      978-1-63185-054-7
Cooking / Regional & Ethnic / Middle Eastern
14.06.24

TABLE OF CONTENTS

INTRODUCTION

I am a mother. I am a wife. I am a working woman—three unique identities, three very different sets of challenges and responsibilities. Although the roles are different in many ways, they are all expressions of the deepest parts of me, nurtured and sustained by my Jewish faith.

The Bible teaches us that even the most mundane tasks can be elevated to a high spiritual level by our thoughts, actions, and intentions. Food is a good example of this. In Judaism, food is regarded as a gift from God. Food is transformed from a purely physical experience to a spiritual event by the blessings we make before and after we eat or drink anything, and recognizing where our sustenance comes from. The act of blessing and drinking wine and challah is the hallmark of the Sabbath and holiday table. In fact, the family table is a central focus in Judaism, a place where tradition is taught and perpetuated. The family table and the experience of eating together is considered to be so essential to Jewish life that the table is compared to the altar in the ancient Holy Temple in Jerusalem.

Cooking three meals a day, day in and day out, can become drudgery. But it is possible to elevate the act of cooking, to imbue it with great significance. It is possible to use cooking as an opportunity for meditation, self-reflection, and spiritual growth. If we use the time that we're cooking to pray and reflect, that energy flows into the food that we serve our families and our guests.

In this book, I offer biblical verses and my interpretations along with recipes. These are verses that help me bridge the gap between the mundane and the spiritual, verses that help me transform the act of cooking into something meaningful and holy. When I focus on Bible verses and meditation while I cook, cooking is no longer a mundane activity that I dread but rather a prime opportunity to develop my inner being. The act of cooking transforms from the purely mundane into the spiritual.

I have also developed recipes that are simple, healthy, and delicious, and that can easily be doubled and tripled to serve more people. I cook for my family daily and for the many guests we have at our *Shabbat* (Sabbath) table every weekend. By focusing my mind on the purpose of every action, it is easy to find the beauty, and by using these easy and delicious recipes, I can enjoy the preparation as well as the sacred time I spend with my family and my guests.

I invite you to integrate your Bible study and your spiritual life with the very physical act of food preparation. I am certain that, like me, you'll bring renewed energy and enthusiasm to the godly task of feeding and nurturing your family.

With blessings from the Holy Land,
Yael

"THE VIRTUE OF ANGELS IS THAT THEY CANNOT DETERIORATE; THEIR FLAW IS THAT THEY CANNOT IMPROVE. MAN'S FLAW IS THAT HE CAN DETERIORATE; AND HIS VIRTUE IS THAT HE CAN IMPROVE."

—HASIDIC SAYING—

"GOD DWELLS WHEREVER
MAN LETS HIM IN."

—RABBI OF KOTZK—

"PEACE BE TO YOU, FEAR NOT."

GENESIS 43:23

Fear is an enemy that can prevent us from pursuing our dreams and achieving our goals. We all experience fear of failure, ridicule, and disappointment, and that fear can sap our strength, weaken our resolve, and steal our ambition. Recognize your dreams and follow them where they lead. Success is born in the pursuit of dreams, and failure only happens when you give up before you try. Open your heart to the universe and let go of your fears. Enjoy the road and be open to a vast array of destinations; trust that the path will take you to the right place.

SALADS & DIPS

chef salad

CHEF SALAD

I love making this chef salad because of the many ways it highlights the beauty of nature that God created. With its rainbow of colors and flavors, this salad looks beautiful on the table and tastes amazing.

INGREDIENTS

3 cups lettuce
2 carrots, shredded
1 cup purple cabbage, chopped
1 avocado, cubed
1 cup cheddar cheese, shredded
¼ cup raisins
2 tablespoons sesame seeds
2 tablespoons sunflower seeds, salted

CREAMY DRESSING

1 cup mayonnaise
½ small onion
2 tablespoons red wine vinegar
½ tablespoon brown sugar
¼ teaspoon garlic powder
Salt and pepper to taste

- In a blender or food processor, combine all dressing ingredients.

- Pour over salad immediately before serving.

HUMMUS

Hummus is a staple food in Israel which is served at nearly every meal. We dip vegetables in hummus for breakfast, spread it on bread at lunch, and serve it as a side dish for dinner. This delicious and healthy dip is surprisingly easy to make, and stays good in the refrigerator for up to a week.

INGREDIENTS

15-ounce can garbanzo beans, drained and rinsed
⅓ cup tahini paste
4 cloves garlic
½ cup fresh lemon juice *or* to taste
1 tablespoon extra virgin olive oil, plus more for garnish
¾ teaspoon cumin
½ teaspoon salt *or* to taste
Sweet paprika to decorate

- Place all ingredients in a food processor with the blade insert.

- Pulse for 50 seconds, then process until smooth.

- Place the smooth hummus in a shallow bowl. With a spoon create a small well in the middle, fill the well with olive oil, sprinkle with paprika and serve.

"SPEAK TO THE EARTH, AND IT SHALL TEACH THEE."

JOB 12:8

The beautiful harmony of the natural world is one to cherish and learn from. The rain falls and nurtures the fruits, plants and vegetables, animals are fed, human life is sustained. The cycle of nature is an ecosystem that, when undisturbed, is a chain that provides for all. Take a moment to recognize the journey taken by the water in our cup and the food on our plate and open yourself up to amazement and appreciation. We have the same ability to provide sustenance to others by sharing a nice word, a kind smile, or a nutritious meal. Find your way to give to others!

COLE SLAW

This is one salad that I always have in my fridge. I make the shredded vegetable mix and salad dressing, and then keep them separate until right before I'm ready to serve it. This traditional Jewish salad is simple—yet delicious—and goes well with everything. It is a good accompaniment to both meat and dairy meals, and is great as a healthy snack any time of day.

INGREDIENTS

½ head purple cabbage, shredded
½ head white cabbage, shredded
2 carrots, shredded

- Mix vegetables together.

DRESSING

4 tablespoons mayonnaise
2 tablespoons mustard
1 tablespoon sugar
1 tablespoon rice vinegar
1 tablespoon lemon juice
½ teaspoon soy sauce
Salt and pepper to taste

- Blend together the dressing ingredients.

- Combine salad and dressing right before serving.

COLORFUL LETTUCE

This is a quick salad that I whip up at the last minute when I have many guests coming over and I become concerned that I need more food. This salad takes just a few minutes to prepare and has only a few ingredients, yet it looks and tastes delicious.

INGREDIENTS

4 cups mixed baby lettuce
1 cup purple cabbage, chopped
1 carrot, shredded
1 red pepper, chopped
1 avocado, cubed
½ cup chickpeas from a can, drained

- Mix together all ingredients; pour dressing onto the salad immediately before serving.

SALAD DRESSING

3 tablespoons extra virgin olive oil
1½ tablespoons balsamic vinegar
1 teaspoon honey
1 teaspoon Dijon mustard
1 teaspoon mayonnaise
Salt and pepper to taste

- Place all ingredients together in a jar and shake well.

"THE PRICE OF WISDOM IS ABOVE RUBIES."

JOB 28:18

Happiness cannot be purchased, and cannot be achieved through material wealth. A person is happy who is content with the blessings he has. A person who finds happiness from within himself will rise to every challenge of life. One who recognizes God in his life, who is able to see the beauty of God all around him, will never feel alone.

EGG SALAD

In my house, egg salad is the one dish that I know all three of my picky kids will eat. My neighbor has a chicken coop in his yard, so I often take my kids to the coop and find fresh eggs that we go home to cook and eat. There are so many variations of egg salad, but this recipe is my family's favorite.

INGREDIENTS

4 eggs, hard boiled
2 tablespoons mayonnaise
¼ cup onions, chopped
½ teaspoon salt
Pepper
½ teaspoon sweet paprika

- Mash the hard-boiled eggs.

- One by one, add the remaining ingredients in the order listed.

Delicious on a cracker or sandwich, and a side dish that goes with everything!

delicious seed mix

DELICIOUS SEED MIX

This mix is my husband's invention, the source of my "seed mix" addiction. This seed mix tastes delicious on everything; I sprinkle it on all my salads, mix it into rice dishes, eat it on bread with a little butter, and even top my breakfast eggs with these seeds. The mixture stays good for a long time, so sometimes we will make double or triple the recipe…it always gets eaten in the end!

INGREDIENTS

⅓ cup pumpkin seeds
¼ cup sunflower seeds
2 tablespoons flax seeds
1 tablespoon white sesame seeds
1 tablespoon black sesame seeds

- Warm up a medium-sized pan over medium heat (without oil).

- Place all the seeds in the pan over a low flame, mix constantly for 3-5 minutes, until the seeds are turning a light brown color.

- Sprinkle a little salt on the seeds and mix (optional).

- Before serving, mix a little olive oil with the seeds (optional).

Store in Tupperware for up to two weeks, and sprinkle the seed mixture over salads, on sandwiches, and on any of your favorite dishes.

israeli salad

israeli salad
with seed mix

ISRAELI SALAD

My husband is Israeli and I remember being at his parents' house and offering to help his mother make a salad. She sent me to the fridge to get out the vegetables and when I saw there was no lettuce in the vegetable drawer I was totally confused. "How will we make a salad without lettuce?" I asked her, dumbfounded. Well, apparently Israeli salads are lettuce-free! The trick to an Israeli salad is to take lots of vegetables and chop them up very small, then top them with a simple olive oil dressing. It is a staple of the Israeli meal. You'll never believe how delicious (and colorful!) this wonderful salad comes out.

INGREDIENTS

2 cucumbers
2 carrots
2 pickles
1 red pepper
1 scallion stalk
Parsley, chopped (optional)

DRESSING

¼ cup olive oil
Juice from half a fresh lemon
Salt and pepper to taste

- Finely chop all the vegetables and place in a bowl.

- Mix together the salad dressing, and pour onto the salad immediately before serving.

PESTO

This traditional Italian dip is popular in the Middle East. Our *Shabbat* meals always begin with a salad course that includes a number of dips, of which pesto is one of our favorites. It is a good dip for challah, vegetables, and of course, is perfect for pesto pasta. Yummmm, delicious!

INGREDIENTS

   1 large bunch basil, leaves only, washed and dried
   3 medium cloves garlic
   ½ cup pine nuts
   ¼ cup sunflower seeds
   ½ cup parmesan cheese, loosely packed and freshly grated (optional)
   ¼ cup extra virgin olive oil

   • Put all ingredients in a food processor, and blend until it is all mixed together and smooth.

"DEPART FROM EVIL, AND DO GOOD; SEEK PEACE, AND PURSUE IT."

PSALM 34:14

A meaningful life is a life of purpose and intention. We must do good, seek peace, and actively pursue the things in life that matter. Nothing of value just happens. We must be active participants in the drama of living well. What matters to you most? What is of ultimate value? Never stop working on yourself and striving toward more conscious living. It is the examined life that leads toward fulfillment and joy.

SHREDDED BEET & CARROT SALAD

I always serve colorful and healthy salads before the main course. I never mind if my kids fill up on a healthy appetizer! This salad has beautiful colors and looks lovely on the table. It's quick and easy to prepare.

INGREDIENTS

3 carrots
2 beets
2 celery stalks
2 tablespoons olive oil
1 tablespoon lemon juice
Salt and pepper to taste

- In a food processor, with shredder insert, shred beets and carrots.

- Chop the celery stalks by hand and mix together with beet and carrot mixture.

- Dress the salad immediately before serving with olive oil, lemon juice, salt, and pepper.

Spinach & Strawberry Salad

This salad always makes me think of summer, even if I'm serving it in the dead of winter. Who doesn't like strawberries in their salad? This salad is sweet and delicious, and is the perfect way to get those picky eaters to get their healthy serving of spinach.

INGREDIENTS

1 pound fresh spinach
1 pint strawberries, sliced
1 cup pecans, sugared
½ red onion, sliced

DRESSING

¾ cup sugar
⅓ cup vinegar
¼ cup poppy seeds
1 teaspoon salt
1½ tablespoons onion, grated
1 teaspoon dry mustard
1 cup olive oil

- Combine spinach, pecans, onions, and strawberries in bowl.

- In a blender, mix sugar, vinegar, poppy seeds, salt, dry mustard, and onion. Slowly add the oil. Pour over salad.

"SO TEACH US TO NUMBER OUR DAYS, THAT WE MAY APPLY OUR HEARTS UNTO WISDOM."

PSALM 90:12

Try to savor each moment and appreciate the people around you and the task you are engaged in. Think about what you are doing. Every moment of your life is precious. Each day is a blessing from God, an opportunity to grow in wisdom and faith and to fill your world with kindness. There is no such thing as mundane; with the proper intention and thoughts, we can lift almost any action up to holiness.

SWEET & SALTY
SPINACH SALAD

I love salads based on spinach, and I can't resist anything with cheese. If you feel the same, you'll love this salad.

INGREDIENTS

4 cups fresh spinach leaves
1 tangerine, cut into small pieces
¼ cup sunflower seeds, salted
¼ cup cranberries
1 whole avocado, cubed
¼ cup crumbled feta cheese (optional)

DRESSING

1½ tablespoons balsamic vinegar
3 tablespoons extra virgin olive oil
1 teaspoon honey
1 tablespoon brown sugar
1 teaspoon Dijon mustard
Salt and pepper to taste

- Place all ingredients in a jar and mix well.

TAHINI

Prepared tahini is available at every supermarket, yet it doesn't compare in taste to fresh, homemade tahini, which takes only minutes to prepare. This tahini will last for around a week in the fridge, but the raw tahini stays good for months. Tahini is a real Israeli food that you can easily prepare in your own kitchen.

INGREDIENTS

½ cup raw tahini
¾ cup water
Juice from half a fresh lemon
1 clove garlic, crushed
1 teaspoon ground cumin powder
¼ teaspoon salt

- In a medium-sized bowl, mix together the raw tahini and water for 2 minutes. (It will be liquid, then thick, and if you continue mixing it will get to a perfect consistency.)

- Add the remaining ingredients, mix, and serve.

Tahina is delicious as a dip for bread, on salad, or as a dip for vegetables. It is a staple food in Israel that we put on everything!

"ON THREE THINGS THE WORLD IS SUSTAINED: ON THE TORAH, ON THE (TEMPLE) SERVICE, AND ON DEEDS OF LOVING KINDNESS."

ETHICS OF THE FATHERS, CHAPTER 1

Ancient Jewish wisdom establishes life's priorities. Our obligation is to study and to live God's Word, to serve God, and to perform good deeds. The Ten Commandments are composed of five that pertain to the relationship between man and God, and five that pertain to the relationship between man and man. The spiritual and physical realms are of importance to God, and in order to serve God, we are obliged to nurture both aspects.

"BUT THEY THAT WAIT UPON THE LORD SHALL RENEW THEIR STRENGTH; THEY SHALL MOUNT UP WITH WINGS AS EAGLES; THEY SHALL RUN, AND NOT BE WEARY, THEY SHALL WALK, AND NOT FAINT."

ISAIAH 40:31

True strength comes from faith in the Lord. It is easy to confuse strength with other things, like power, wealth, and success. But that type of strength is fragile and ephemeral. It comes and it goes, it disappoints. Faith in God sustains us through life and survives life's challenges. Only faith in God gives strength that can heal, power to conquer our fears, and the stamina to pursue our dreams. It's the kind of strength that grows with age and doesn't diminish.

TOMATO MOZZARELLA SALAD

This simple salad is so quick to prepare and is unbelievably delicious. I love eating it for a light lunch throughout the week. I grow my own basil in our garden, and my kids love picking the basil leaves from the plant and putting them directly into the salad.

INGREDIENTS

15 cherry tomatoes, halved
10 leaves fresh basil
5 black olives, halved and pitted
½ cup mozzarella, cubed

- Mix together in a bowl or set out nicely on a serving plate.

DRESSING

1 tablespoon olive oil
½ tablespoon balsamic vinegar
Salt and pepper to taste

- Mix the dressing together, then pour over the salad immediately before serving.

> ## "KNOW THEREFORE THAT THE LORD THY GOD, HE IS GOD, THE FAITHFUL GOD, WHICH KEEPETH COVENANT AND MERCY WITH THEM THAT LOVE HIM AND KEEP HIS COMMANDMENTS TO A THOUSAND GENERATIONS."
>
> ### DEUTERONOMY 7:9

God's Word is eternal and He will be faithful forever to those who love Him and live by His Word. His presence is not always obvious. There are times that He feels hidden and we feel alone. It is for us to establish God's presence in our heart and in the world. Do something for someone else, help someone out, give of yourself—see how quickly you feel His presence all around you.

GRAINS & SIDES

"THE NAME OF THE LORD IS A STRONG TOWER: THE RIGHTEOUS RUNNETH INTO IT AND IS SAFE."

PROVERBS 18:10

Bricks and mortar may hold the promise of safety, but true protection comes only from God. A secure life is not achieved by anything that money can buy or man can build. Only by calling on the name of the Lord will we have that "strong tower;" only when we incorporate God into our lives will we know His name to call.

ASIAN BROWN RICE

INGREDIENTS

1 tablespoon ginger, chopped
5 cloves garlic, chopped
Oil for sautéing
1 cup brown rice
2 cups water
¼ cup canned corn
¼ cup canned peas
½ teaspoon salt
1 tablespoon toasted sesame oil

- In a medium-sized pot, sauté chopped ginger and garlic in oil.

- Add brown rice and water.

- Once it is boiling, put in corn, peas, and salt. Cover.

- Simmer and cook rice until water is absorbed.

- Add toasted sesame oil.

BAKED EGG ROLLS

Seriously…who doesn't like egg rolls? I love egg rolls, but up until one of my friends shared this special recipe with me, it was a guilty pleasure. These egg rolls are baked, not fried, and taste amazing!

INGREDIENTS

1 package Moroccan cigar filo dough
2 cups each shredded cabbage and carrots
3 cups sprouts of your choice
2 tablespoons vinegar
3 tablespoons oil
2 tablespoons soy sauce
1 tablespoon honey

- Preheat oven to 375°F.

- Sauté veggies together in oil. Add vinegar, soy sauce, and honey to the sautéed vegetables.

- Place cooked vegetables on dough and roll up into an egg roll.

- Bake at 375°F for approximately 15 minutes or until golden brown.

"FOR I KNOW THE THOUGHTS I THINK TOWARD YOU, SAITH THE LORD, THOUGHTS OF PEACE, AND NOT OF EVIL, TO GIVE YOU AN EXPECTED END."

JEREMIAH 29:11

When we are going through difficult times, it can feel like God has forgotten or abandoned us. Throughout our hardships, we must try to remember that God is in control and and has a master plan. When you wake up in the morning and before you go to sleep, remind yourself that you are dear to God and that He is with you during every moment of every day. Next time things do not go your way or you receive difficult news, take a moment to remember this verse and feel in your heart that God has a divine plan.

BROCCOLI CASSEROLE

INGREDIENTS

½ bag frozen broccoli, thawed
1½ tablespoons olive oil
1½ tablespoons flour
3 eggs
½ cup mayonnaise
2 tablespoons onion soup mix *or* one sautéed onion
½ teaspoon salt
½ cup soy milk
1 cup corn flakes
½ cup honey

- Preheat oven to 375°F.

- Mix all ingredients (other than corn flakes and honey) and pour into greased pan.

- Cover the top with crushed corn flakes and drizzle with honey.

- Bake for 45 minutes at 375°F.

BULGAR TABOULI

This recipe makes a great light lunch that can be prepared a day in advance. It's one of my husband's favorites.

INGREDIENTS

1 cup raw bulgar
1 cup lemon juice
⅔ cup olive oil
5 cloves garlic, crushed
Salt and pepper to taste
6-8 scallions, chopped
2 handfuls parsley
⅓ cup mint, chopped
5 tomatoes, with seeds removed

- Mix together bulgar, lemon juice, olive oil, garlic, salt, and pepper.

- Add scallions, parsley, mint, tomatoes.

- Let sit in fridge until the bulgar gets soft...then serve!

carrot kugel bread

CARROT KUGEL BREAD

I serve this carrot bread with the meal as a side dish, yet it truly tastes like dessert. You can decide – side or dessert?

INGREDIENTS

2 cups flour
1½ cup sugar
2 teaspoons baking powder
1 teaspoon baking soda
1 teaspoon cinnamon
3 carrots, shredded
⅔ cup orange juice
3 tablespoons lemon juice
4 eggs
1 teaspoons salt

- Preheat oven to 350°F.

- Mix all ingredients together and pour in greased loaf pan.

- Bake at 350°F for 50-60 minutes (until a toothpick comes out clean when you stick it in the middle).

COCONUT MILK RICE

The creamy texture and mixture of tastes makes this recipe one of the most delicious rice dishes I have ever tasted.

INGREDIENTS

2 cups basmati rice
2 cups coconut cream or canned coconut liquid
2 cups water
1 tablespoon tumeric powder
½ teaspoon garlic powder
¼ cup fresh dill, chopped
2 cinnamon sticks
Salt and pepper

- Put all ingredients together in a pot, bring to a boil, then cover and simmer until water is absorbed and rice is soft (around 10 minutes).

- After the rice is cooked, top with a little bit of soy sauce and enjoy!

"BE STRONG AND OF GOOD COURAGE, FEAR NOT NOR BE AFRAID OF THEM: FOR THE LORD THY GOD, HE IT IS THAT DOTH GO WITH THEE; HE WILL NOT FAIL THEE, NOR FORSAKE THEE."

DEUTERONOMY 31:6

Sometimes it seems as if tragedy is everywhere and it can sap our courage and strength. When you turn to God and keep Him in your heart and mind, you will know that you are not alone. When you keep company with God, you walk without fear.

"THY WORD IS A LAMP UNTO MY FEET, AND A LIGHT UNTO MY PATH."

PSALM 119:105

Through our speech we have the ability to change someone's entire reality. When you see someone is sad, tell them nice things. Say, "Hello" next time you throw a dollar into a beggar's cup. Teach your children a trade that they enjoy. Explain your intentions to a person you annoy. Speak out loud to yourself to overcome your problems, confusion, and worry. Light your own path, along with others, through the power of speech.

CREAMY & CHEESY POTATOES

Cheesy potatoes is definitely on my list of "top 5 favorite foods" and I've been testing out different recipes to make this mouthwateringly delicious dish perfect. Get your fingers ready for licking!

INGREDIENTS

8 medium potatoes
1 (12-ounce) can coconut milk or liquid
Salt and pepper to taste
Paprika to taste
2 cups shredded cheddar cheese

- Preheat oven to 450°F.

- Cut potatoes in small, thin pieces and pour coconut milk over them. Top with salt, pepper, and paprika.

- Bake covered at 450°F for around 35 minutes or until the potatoes are soft.

- Take the potatoes out of the oven and sprinkle shredded cheddar cheese on top; bake uncovered for another 10 minutes.

PARSLEY & GARLIC GREEN BEANS

INGREDIENTS

2 pounds fresh green beans *or* 1 (12-ounce) frozen package
1 cup water
1 head garlic, chopped
1 tablespoon oil
½ teaspoon salt
⅛ teaspoon pepper
1 cup fresh parsley, chopped

- Wash green beans, trim ends and remove any strings.

- Bring water to a boil in large saucepan. Add beans.

- Cover, reduce heat to medium, and cook 10 minutes, stirring occasionally.

- Drain and set aside.

- While you're waiting for the beans to cook, warm up the oil in a large skillet.

- Once oil is warm, add garlic and cook until soft (4 minutes); add the green beans. Stir in parsley, salt, and pepper. Cook over medium heat 3 minutes or until thoroughly heated, stirring occasionally.

- Serve and enjoy!

PESTO BASMATI

INGREDIENTS

1 cup basmati rice, cooked
¼ cup pesto
½ cup parmesan cheese, shredded

• Mix all ingredients together.

Tip: See page 22 for recipe on making your own pesto.

yellow rice

Yellow Rice

I often have lots of big families with kids over for *Shabbat* meals and need a simple dish that is easy to prepare and feeds many. This plain rice dish is simple enough that the picky kids like it, yet sophisticated enough that the adults will enjoy it as well. It's a great side for any meal, and adds some color to your table.

INGREDIENTS

1 tablespoon tumeric
¼ teaspoon salt
2 cups basmati rice
4 cups water

- Combine tumeric, salt, (uncooked) rice, and water.

- Bring to a boil, cover, and simmer until water is absorbed (around 10 minutes).

POTATO (KUGEL) CASSEROLE

Potato kugel is a traditional side dish for *Shabbat* lunch meals. It's delicious straight from the oven, and reheats beautifully the next day.

INGREDIENTS

6 large white potatoes
2 large onions
4 eggs, lightly beaten
¼ cup oil
3 teaspoons salt
¼ teaspoon pepper
2 tablespoons oil

- Preheat oven to 400°F.

- Grate potatoes with onions. Drain liquid.

- Add eggs and stir in oil (¼ cup); mix together.

- Add salt and pepper; mix together.

- In medium-sized pan, add oil (2 tablespoons) and heat in oven at 400°F for one minute.

- Take out hot pan and pour in the potato mixture. Bake uncovered at 400°F for 1 hour, until the top is slightly crispy and golden brown.

"FOR MY BRETHREN AND COMPANIONS' SAKES, I WILL NOW SAY, PEACE BE WITH IN THEE."

PSALM 122:8

Our central focus is on our own lives, problems, and thoughts, yet it is crucial to open up and think about others. It can sometimes be a challenge to truly feel happiness for someone else's success and to help them reach their goals, yet it brings completion to the heart. We are all connected in good times and bad and have the power to change someone's hardships into blessings through nice words, guidance, and intention. Go out and change the world through the power of words! Bring peace to the universe!

"I PUT ON RIGHTEOUSNESS, AND IT CLOTHED ME."

JOB 29:14

We wear our values like our clothes – they cover us, they protect us, they define us. What garments do you want the world to see? Choose your values no less carefully than you choose the clothing you wear each day. Stay focused and alert to ensure that your actions clothe you in beauty and righteousness.

DAIRY & VEGAN MAIN COURSES

CHAPATI WRAPS

Chapati wraps are similar to soft tortilla wraps, and are traditionally served in Israel in place of bread. They take just a few minutes to prepare and taste delicious when stuffed with nearly anything and used as a wrap. I like cutting up lots of fresh vegetables and preparing homemade dips, setting everything up in bowls on the table, and letting my children fill their own chapati. It's different and fun!

INGREDIENTS

3 cups flour
1 cup warm water
1 teaspoon salt
2-3 teaspoons oil

- Mix all ingredients together and knead on floured surface.

- Roll into round-shaped, flat wraps.

- Warm a medium-sized pan over medium heat, then place the flat wraps in the pan to cook (without oil).

- Cook over medium flame for 2-3 minutes on each side.

"THOU SHALT SHINE FORTH, THOU SHALT BE AS THE MORNING."

JOB 11:17

It is the simple miracles that we must learn to appreciate. The sun rises each morning, replacing the darkness, bringing new possibilities to life. As God in His goodness renews creation each day, we must greet each day with appreciation for the miracle of life and the possibilities that life holds.

"BEHOLD, HOW GOOD AND HOW PLEASANT IT IS FOR BRETHREN TO DWELL TOGETHER IN UNITY!"

PSALM 133:1

Genuine respect for others is possible and attainable. Try to open up your heart to the world and all the different colors, customs, traditions, needs, and aspirations surrounding us. We must not try and change one another, but rather understand, respect, and learn from everyone. Once we realize that each person on this earth is a spark of the infinite, we can appreciate our differences. Try to find a positive point in each person you don't get along with and let that point be your focus. That point is their strength that you can surely learn from.

Cheese Quiche

This is a great recipe to make with children who love to help in the kitchen; my kids enjoy sprinkling the cheese and mixing the ingredients.

Ingredients

    2 cups cottage cheese
    1 cup yogurt, plain and unsweetened
    5 eggs, beaten
    ¼ cup feta cheese, crumbled
    ¼ cup parmesan cheese
    ¼ cup cheddar cheese
    1 pie crust, prepared
    ¼ teaspoon salt
    Pepper
    ½ cup American cheese, grated

- Preheat oven to 400°F.

- Place all ingredients except American cheese in bowl and mix well. Pour mixture into pie crust.

- Top with ½ cup grated American cheese.

- Bake on 400°F for 25 minutes, or until the top is golden brown and the eggs are cooked.

CREAMY LASAGNA

From the time my eldest daughter could talk, she has asked for my lasagna – for breakfast, lunch and dinner! Each time I make this lasagna I think of my daughter, and I integrate good thoughts and prayers into my cooking.

INGREDIENTS

1 cup cottage cheese, small curd
1 cup yogurt, plain and unsweetened
1½ cups sweet creamer
1 (6.5-ounce) jar pasta sauce
½ teaspoon salt
12 pieces lasagna noodles (no need to pre-cook)
4 cups shredded cheese of your choice

- Preheat oven to 400°F.

- In a bowl, mix together all ingredients except for the noodles and shredded cheese.

- In a medium-sized pan, place a layer of sauce, noodles, sauce, ¾ cup shredded cheese. Repeat. Top off the lasagna with 1 cup shredded cheese.

- Bake covered on 400°F for 40 minutes. Uncover and cook for 15 minutes more.

CREAMY PEANUT BUTTER NOODLES

When I went to college in New York there was a local Asian restaurant that made the most delicious peanut butter noodles.

INGREDIENTS

1 (8-ounce) package of spaghetti or rice soba noodles
½ cup peanut butter
3 tablespoons soy sauce
½ teaspoon lemon juice
½ cup vegetable broth
1½ tablespoons brown sugar
¼ teaspoon salt
1 scallion, chopped
2 tablespoons sesame seeds

- Cook rice soba noodles or traditional spaghetti according to package instructions, set aside.

- In a saucepan add together all the ingredients except for the spaghetti, scallions, and sesame seeds.

- Turn flame on low and stir constantly for 2 minutes until all ingredients are mixed together.

- Mix noodles and sauce together. Top with scallions and sesame seeds. Serve hot or cold.

CREAMY VEGETABLE-COCONUT MILK PASTA

Made without milk or cheese, the secret ingredient in this sauce is coconut milk. I know you'll enjoy this unique, guilt-free pasta recipe.

INGREDIENTS

1-pound package spaghetti
4 tablespoons olive oil
½ cup mushrooms, chopped
1 onion, sliced
½ cup broccoli, chopped
6 cherry tomatoes, halved
2 cups canned coconut liquid
Salt and pepper to taste
¼ teaspoon garlic powder

- Cook spaghetti according to instructions and set aside.

- In a big saucepan, heat olive oil, add fresh vegetables and sauté for 10 minutes, stirring often so that they don't stick.

- Add coconut milk and spices to the vegetables and simmer for 10 minutes.

- Pour the sauce over the spaghetti and enjoy!

Can also be served over rice or quinoa.

"HER WAYS ARE WAYS OF PLEASANTNESS, AND ALL HER PATHS ARE PEACE."

PROVERBS 3:17

Peace is a state of being and a state of mind that needs to be cultivated and nurtured. Peace can exist within, independent of the turmoil that surrounds us. Positive thoughts, peaceful ways, and loving deeds lead us toward that place of peace and fulfillment.

CUPCAKE PIZZA CALZONE

When I bite into these pizza calzone cups, I remember why nearly everyone in the world loves pizza…including my three Israeli children. It's not always easy to find good pizza in the Holy Land, so I prepare these pizza calzone "cupcakes." You can add any vegetables you like. I like it spicy, and I often cut up and add a piece of fresh hot chili pepper to the calzone cup.

INGREDIENTS

1 (9-ounce) package filo dough cups/shells
Prepared 32-ounce jar pasta sauce
1 cup feta cheese
2 cups mozzarella cheese, shredded
Fresh mushrooms, sliced or diced
Salt and pepper to taste

- Preheat oven to 275°F.

- In a muffin pan line each cup with filo dough.

- Place one spoonful of pasta sauce inside the filo dough, along with a small piece of feta cheese, shredded mozzarella, and some mushrooms.

- Top with half a spoonful of pasta sauce, and salt and pepper to taste.

- Bake on 275°F until filo dough is brown and crispy and cheese is melted (around 15 minutes).

- Let cool for 5 minutes. Enjoy!

SESAME TOFU SLICES

Tofu takes on the flavor and texture of the ingredients you cook it with. I love crispy tofu with a salty flavor, and sesame seeds on top make it simply delicious! We sometimes use tofu as a topping to a fresh salad. It's versatile – and you can be creative with it!

INGREDIENTS

14 ounces extra firm tofu
¼ cup flour, for dusting
3 tablespoons canola oil, for frying
1 cup sesame seeds, lightly toasted
1 bunch scallions, trimmed and cut into 1-inch pieces

SAUCE

⅓ cup honey
3 tablespoons tamari soy sauce
1 teaspoon ginger powder
2 tablespoons sesame oil

2 tablespoons rice vinegar
2 cloves garlic, finely minced
1 teaspoon red chili pepper flakes

- Wrap tofu with paper towels and drain liquid.

- Cut the tofu into 2-inch by 2-inch squares and set aside.

- Stir sauce ingredients together.

- Dust tofu very lightly with flour, and coat with sauce.

- Heat 1 inch of oil in deep frying pan.

- Fry tofu in oil until golden brown; turn over and cook until both sides are browned.

- Place fried tofu in a large bowl and toss with 1 cup sauce, sprinkle liberally with sesame seeds and scallions and serve hot.

SHAKSHUKA

Shakshuka is a traditional Israeli breakfast – and it is as much of a treat at home as it is in our corner cafe.

INGREDIENTS

1 tablespoon canola oil
1 onion, chopped
1 zucchini, chopped
2 cloves garlic, chopped
2 tomatoes, diced
10-ounce jar pasta sauce
5 eggs

- In a large pan, heat the oil over medium heat.

- Add the onion, zucchini, and garlic; sauté until soft and onions are a little browned.

- Add tomatoes and sauté for another 3 minutes, mixing.

- Add pasta sauce to the vegetable mixture and over a low flame bring to a boil.

- While boiling, crack eggs on top of the mixture. Boil for another 10 minutes until the white part of the egg is cooked. Serve with bread.

Tip: After the eggs are cracked on top of the tomato mixture, use a spatula to make little holes in the tomato mixture to let the white part of the eggs seep through and cook.

Optional: sprinkle feta cheese on top.

HEARTY & DELICIOUS LENTILS

Before making this recipe, it was simply a dream of mine that my children would beg me for healthy food for dinner. This lentil recipe is so hearty and delicious that majadra (lentils and rice) is my children's second favorite food, coming in close after lasagna. I love eating this healthy and tasty dish for lunch or dinner, and leftovers heat up perfectly.

INGREDIENTS

1 tablespoon canola oil
1 onion, sliced
2 carrots, chopped
4 cloves garlic, chopped
2 celery stalks, chopped
½ cup ketchup
1 teaspoon curry
1 tablespoon soy sauce
1 tablespoon brown sugar
1 cup lentils
3 cups water

- In a medium-sized pot, heat canola oil.

- Add onion, carrots, garlic and celery and sauté for 2 minutes.

- Add ketchup, curry, soy sauce, brown sugar, and salt; mix together with vegetables for 2 minutes over medium heat.

- Add lentils and water to the pot with vegetables and sauce, mix together, and bring to a boil. Simmer for an hour, or until lentils are soft. Add more water if needed.

- Serve over brown or white rice and top with feta cheese (optional).

*hearty &
delicious lentils*

veggie noodle stir fry

VEGGIE NOODLE STIR FRY

INGREDIENTS

1 (1-pound) spaghetti noodles, broken in half

4 tablespoons olive oil

2 cups purple cabbage, chopped

2 scallions, chopped

5 cloves garlic, chopped

1 carrot, chopped

1 cup mung bean sprouts

½ teaspoon ginger powder

2 tablespoons soy sauce

1 tablespoon sugar

- Cook spaghetti noodles according to package instructions until they are al dente. Put aside.

- Heat oil in wok and sauté chopped garlic until golden brown.

- Add the cooked noodles and veggies. Simmer on medium heat for 10 minutes, stirring often.

Spinach Cheese Quiche

I love making quiches for dinner, and I even make a few extras during my free time to place in the freezer for a busy day when I have no time to cook a warm meal for my family. This quiche recipe always comes out perfectly, and is a great way to sneak in the important vitamins from spinach.

INGREDIENTS

2 cups cottage cheese
1 cup yogurt, plain
5 eggs, beat together
1 onion, sliced
3 tablespoons pine nuts
½ cup frozen spinach, thawed and drained
¼ cup feta cheese, crumbled
¼ teaspoon salt
Pepper
1 pie crust, prepared
1 cup mozzarella cheese, grated

- Preheat oven to 400°F.

- Add all ingredients except mozzarella cheese together in a bowl and mix well.

- Pour the mixture into the pie crust.

- Top with grated mozzarella cheese.

- Bake at 400°F for 25 minutes, or until the top is golden brown and the eggs are cooked.

"I HAD RATHER BE A DOORKEEPER IN THE HOUSE OF MY GOD."

PSALM 84:10

Value today is judged in terms of financial worth, and a successful person is defined as one who has achieved great wealth. Redefine the meaning of success for yourself in terms of the joy something brings you, the peace you feel in your heart, and the happiness that accompanies your every step. Choose a profession based on your passions and joys and hang around people who accentuate your good points, who make you laugh and help you feel good.

"BETTER IS A DINNER OF HERBS WHERE LOVE IS, THAN A STALLED OX AND HATRED THEREWITH."

PROVERBS 15:17

The outcome of our toil is based on the intentions that we fill it with. If you are content within yourself and surroundings, joy and tranquility will follow you through all the journeys of your life. When you toil with positive thinking, love, and an open heart, there is no such thing as failure. Failure, anger, and hatred are all relative and based on your state of mind. Put loving intentions into everything you do, stay positive, and when something breaks, pick up the pieces. Failure will be a thing of the past. Simplicity and love are two godly values that can guide our way to true accomplishment and joy.

CHICKEN

bursting with flavor
traditional chicken & potatoes

BURSTING WITH FLAVOR
TRADITIONAL
CHICKEN & POTATOES

Chicken and potatoes is a traditional *Shabbat* main course for Jewish families around the world. This simple dish became a staple *Shabbat* food in Eastern Europe, where potatoes were easy to grow. To this day, Jews around the world continue to make this special dish. This is a delicious and flavorful dish that takes little time to prepare. You can serve the chicken and potatoes together or in separate serving pieces.

INGREDIENTS

1 whole chicken, cut into 8 pieces
4 white potatoes, cubed
1 onion, sliced
1½ tablespoons paprika
1½ tablespoons garlic powder
½ teaspoon salt
Pinch of pepper
1 cup olive oil

- Preheat oven to 425°F.

- Place the chicken with all the ingredients in a cooking bag and shake together.

- Place the closed chicken bag in large baking dish.

- Bake at 425°F for 1 hour. Turn the cooking bag over after 30 minutes.

CHICKEN TERIYAKI

The mix of soy sauce and honey is one of my favorite flavors. When I'm rushed for time yet want to make a special main course that everyone loves – including professional colleagues, my husband, and my three picky kids – this is my go-to recipe.

INGREDIENTS

5 pieces boneless and halved chicken breasts
¼ cup canola oil
½ cup soy sauce
½ cup honey
4 cloves garlic, crushed
2 teaspoons lemon juice
1 tablespoon sesame seeds

- Preheat oven to 375°F.

- In a medium-sized cooking dish, lay out the pieces of chicken.

- Mix together all ingredients except for the sesame seeds and pour over the chicken.

- Cook in oven uncovered for 10 minutes.

- Turn over the chicken pieces and spinkle the sesame seeds on top, continue cooking for another 15 minutes.

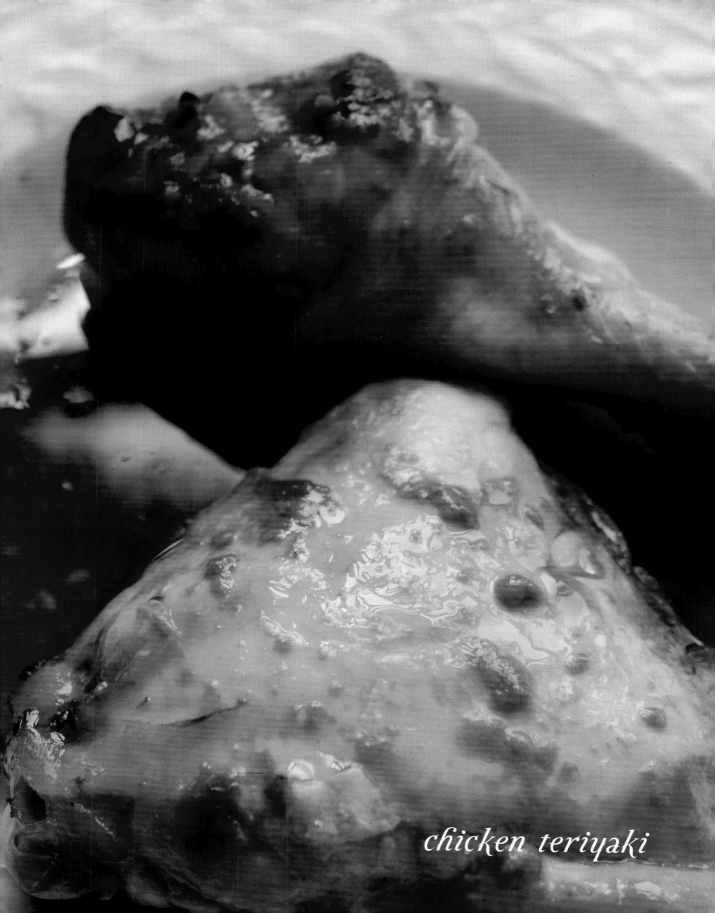

chicken teriyaki

DELICIOUS CREAMY CHICKEN STEW

I keep a strictly kosher home, which means that I never cook with meat and milk together. In this creamy chicken dish, I substitute coconut milk for cream, and the result is just as tasty. This stew is a fun food that my kids love to eat over rice.

INGREDIENTS

1½ tablespoons oil
4 cloves garlic, chopped
1 onion, diced
5 boneless chicken breasts, cut into 1-inch pieces
1 (28-ounce) can diced tomatoes, drained
1 (19-ounce) can chickpeas, drained
1 (19-ounce) can coconut cream/liquid
1 teaspoon salt
1 teaspoon curry
1 teaspoon soy sauce

- In a large saucepan, heat oil.

- Sauté garlic and onion, until onion is clear.

- Add chicken and sauté for another 2-3 minutes until the outside of the chicken is white.

- Add tomatoes, chickpeas, coconut cream, salt, curry, and soy sauce; mix.

- Cover and simmer for 20 minutes, mixing every 5 minutes.

- Serve hot over white basmati rice.

CHICKEN STIR FRY WITH TERIYAKI SAUCE

This delicious stir fry with fresh ginger and garlic is bursting with flavor, and is a perfect alternative to Chinese take-out. It also warms up very well, so save those leftovers!

INGREDIENTS

2 tablespoons canola oil
4 cloves garlic, chopped
1 tablespoon ginger, freshly chopped
1 onion, sliced
3 skinless, boneless chicken breast halves, thinly sliced
4 cups frozen broccoli, thawed
4 tablespoons soy sauce
2 teaspoons brown sugar
Salt and pepper

- In a large saucepan or wok, warm canola oil.

- Add garlic, ginger, and onion; sauté on medium flame while stirring until onion is soft (around 5 minutes).

- Add 3 skinless, boneless chicken breast halves, which have been thinly sliced, and sauté for 3-5 minutes, until the outside of the chicken looks white and cooked.

- Add broccoli, soy sauce, brown sugar, and salt to taste; mix.

- Leave stir fry over flame for another 10-15 minutes, or until the chicken is cooked through.

- Can be served alone or over rice.

"PLEASANT WORDS ARE AS A HONEYCOMB, SWEET TO THE SOUL, AND HEALTH TO THE BONES."

PROVERBS 16:24

When you are happy or love someone, express it. Use your words to create positivity in the world and model the importance of communication and expression. Often we boldly express our concern, anger, or disappointment during difficult times, yet forget to express our joy, thanksgiving, and excitement. Putting feelings into words makes them real and gives everyone around you the gift of sharing your deepest emotions. You will glow with joy after telling a loved one what they mean to you, a parent how much you care, a child how proud you are of them, or a stranger how beautiful their smile is. Give it a try!

HONEY BAKED CHICKEN

This honey chicken is a sweet variation of the traditional Israeli "schnitzel" or fried chicken, yet it is battered and baked instead of fried. Whenever my mother would make this dish, we would all go back to the baking dish with our spoon and take extra sweet corn flake sauce. Now, my children do the same thing when I make this sweet and hearty chicken.

INGREDIENTS

6 bone-in pieces chicken
2 cups canola oil
2 cups lightly seasoned corn flake crumbs
1 cup honey

- Preheat oven to 350°F.

- Dip chicken pieces into a bowl of oil, and then coat with lightly seasoned corn flake crumbs.

- Bake uncovered at 350°F for 30 minutes.

- Drizzle honey over the chicken then continue baking until done (another 15-20 minutes depending on size).

HONEY MUSTARD CHICKEN

This is my husband's favorite chicken dish. I love making it because it takes hardly any time to prepare and I always have the ingredients in the fridge. There are rarely any leftovers, yet when there are, I take the chicken off the bone and throw it in a salad for chicken salad the next day.

INGREDIENTS

3 chicken breast halves
3 chicken drumsticks
¼ cup mustard
½ cup mayonnaise
Juice from one lemon
¼ cup honey
3 cloves garlic, crushed
¼ cup olive oil
Salt to taste
3 tablespoons oil

- Preheat oven to 375°F.

- Mix all ingredients together and pour over chicken.

- Bake uncovered for 30 minutes at 375°F. Baste chicken in sauce after 15 minutes.

JUICY WHOLE CHICKEN

When I was growing up in Chicago, my mother used to make this recipe with turkey. Here in Israel it is nearly impossible to find turkey, so I tried her recipe with chicken and it is equally delicious. This recipe produces the softest and juiciest chicken, and leftovers warm up beautifully.

INGREDIENTS

1 cup chicken broth
1 (4-pound) whole chicken, rinsed and patted dry
½ cup margarine, cut into 1 tablespoon-sized pieces
2 navel oranges, halved

Salt and pepper to taste
2 cloves garlic, minced
½ cup margarine, melted
Paprika

- Preheat oven to 350°F. Pour a little chicken broth into a small roasting pan and set aside.

- Loosen the skin from the breasts and thighs of the chicken. Stuff the margarine pieces evenly underneath the skin of the chicken and place into the roasting pan.

- Squeeze the orange halves over the chicken. Rub in the minced garlic, then sprinkle the chicken with paprika, salt and pepper to taste. Drizzle the melted margarine all over the chicken

- Cover the dish in a loose dome with aluminum foil, and bake in the preheated oven for 20 minutes.

- Uncover and baste the chicken with the pan juices. Continue cooking until the chicken is no longer pink, or until a meat thermometer inserted into the thickest part of the thigh reads 165°F, about 1 to 2 hours. Baste the chicken every 10 minutes after you uncover it.

- Once cooked, allow the chicken to rest out of the oven for 10 minutes before slicing.

MOMMA'S ASIAN CHICKEN NOODLE SALAD

Another favorite childhood dish from growing up in Chicago is my mother's Asian chicken noodle salad. To this day, when I go back to my mom's house, this is the special dish that I ask her to make.

INGREDIENTS

1 (19-ounce) can chicken broth
2 cups water
1 (3-pound) boneless chicken, white meat only, broiled, grilled, or baked and cut up

DRESSING

¼ cup Asian sesame oil
¼ cup vegetable oil
2 tablespoons soy sauce
2 tablespoons brown sugar
½ teaspoons salt
½ teaspoons pepper

SALAD

1 red pepper, cut into fine strips
1 yellow pepper, cut into fine strips
1½ cups cabbage, diced
⅓ cup carrot, diced
1 cup celery, diced
12 snow pea pods
½ pound linguine, cooked

GARNISH

½ cup green onions
1 tablespoon sesame seeds, roasted

- Mix the salad together, top with chicken (hot or cold), pour dressing over it, and garnish.

"THERE IS NOTHING BETTER FOR A MAN, THAN THAT HE SHOULD EAT AND DRINK, AND THAT HE SHOULD MAKE HIS SOUL ENJOY GOOD IN HIS LABOR."

ECCLESIASTES 2:24

We must put pleasure and intention back into the simple things in life. Take a moment to think about the fruit, vegetables, water, and food that we ingest and where they originally came from—the earth. With everything being so complex in this technological era, don't disconnect from the royalty of the earth and the riches it gives us. Find happiness and completion in simple, seemingly mundane acts like eating and drinking.

middle eastern sweet fruit chicken

MIDDLE EASTERN SWEET FRUIT CHICKEN

In the yard of my house we have a beautiful orange tree, walnut tree, and mango tree that we care for and love. During harvest season, I put these fresh fruits and nuts into nearly every dish and thank God for the bounty that He creates.

INGREDIENTS

3 bone-in chicken breast halves and 3 chicken drumsticks
1 cup fresh orange juice *or* juice from 1 orange
½ cup olive oil
1 cup date honey
¼ cup dried cranberries
8 dates, halved and pitted
½ cup walnuts
¼ cup almonds, slivered
1 teaspoon garlic powder
2 tablespoons brown sugar
¼ teaspoon cinnamon
Salt to taste

- Preheat oven to 400°F.

- Place the chicken in a medium-sized baking dish and pour the orange juice over it.

- Cover the raw chicken with olive oil and date honey. (You can buy date honey at a specialty Middle Eastern food store or make it yourself. Recipe is on next page.)

- On top and in between the pieces of chicken, sprinkle dried cranberries, fresh halved dates, walnuts, and slivered almonds.

- Over the chicken mixture, sprinkle salt, pepper, garlic powder, brown sugar, and cinnamon.

- Bake covered at 400°F for 45 minutes to an hour.

- Uncover and baste the chicken with sauce. Cook uncovered for an additional 10 minutes.

DATE HONEY RECIPE
Makes one cup of date honey

8 dates, make sure you buy the fat, sticky Medjool dates
Juice from half a fresh lemon, remove the seeds
½ cup water
½ cup sugar

- Remove the pits from the dates; quarter the dates.

- Mash the dates with a fork into a paste-like consistency.

- Put the mashed dates into a small sauce pan.

- Add the lemon juice and water and heat over a low flame, stirring frequently with a wooden spoon (about 3 minutes).

- After the water is absorbed, add the sugar. The mash should take on a slightly more liquid quality.

- Continue stirring, adding small amounts of water and sugar until you reach a thick consistency.

Sweet & Savory Apricot Mustard Chicken

This savory chicken dish features the unique flavor blend of apricot jelly, brown sugar, and mustard. It is a sure crowd-pleaser for any occasion.

INGREDIENTS

6-8 pieces bone-in chicken (legs, thighs, and/or breast)
½ cup canola oil
¼ cup soy sauce
1½ tablespoons mustard
4 tablespoons apricot jelly
1 teaspoon lemon juice
2 tablespoons brown sugar

- Preheat oven to 375°F.

- Mix together all the ingredients and pour over chicken in a medium-sized baking dish.

- Cook for 45 minutes uncovered, and baste chicken in the sauce halfway through.

*sweet & creamy
peanut butter chicken*

Sweet & Creamy Peanut Butter Chicken

My children eat peanut butter with everything. They take peanut butter sandwiches to school, they dip vegetables in peanut butter for snack time, and they even put peanut butter in cookies and cakes that I bake. I finally succeeded in creating a flavorful chicken recipe that satisfies my children's love for peanut butter, my craving for soy sauce, and my husband's sweet tooth. See if this doesn't please the peanut-butter lovers in your family.

INGREDIENTS

8 pieces bone-in chicken (legs, thighs, and/or breasts)
½ cup olive oil
½ cup peanut butter
1½ tablespoons soy sauce
1 teaspoon lemon juice
1 teaspoon garlic powder *or* crushed garlic
1 teaspoon salt
3 tablespoons brown sugar
1 tablespoon sesame seeds

- Preheat oven to 375°F.

- Mix together all sauce ingredients (except sesame seeds) and pour sauce over chicken in a medium-sized baking dish.

- Top with sesame seeds.

- Bake at 375°F uncovered for 25-30 minutes. Baste chicken in sauce after 15 minutes and continue cooking.

SWEET VEGETABLE CHICKEN

This chicken comes out juicy and perfect and the extra vegetable sauce tastes great on rice or as a dip with bread. One of the highlights of my week is going vegetable shopping at the local farmers market. I try to incorporate many of the fresh vegetables I've purchased into our daily menu, and this chicken dish has become a family staple. You can use whatever vegetables are fresh and in season for this dish.

INGREDIENTS

6-8 pieces bone-in chicken breast
2 heads garlic, cloved
2 tomatoes, diced
3 celery stalks, chopped
1 zucchini, chopped
1 onion, sliced
1 sweet potato, thinly sliced
4 tablespoons balsamic vinegar
½ cup brown sugar
1 tablespoon mustard
¼ cup olive oil

- Preheat oven to 375°F.

- In a large baking dish, lay out the chicken one piece next to the other.

- Place all the vegetables and garlic on top and around the chicken.

- Mix together the balsamic vinegar, brown sugar, mustard, and olive oil and pour over the chicken and vegetables.

- Bake uncovered at 375°F for 20-25 minutes. Baste the chicken in the sauce after 15 minutes.

- Serve alone or with basmati rice.

"MY SOUL SHALL BE SATISFIED AS WITH MARROW AND FATNESS; AND MY MOUTH SHALL PRAISE THEE WITH JOYFUL LIPS."

PSALM 63:5

As delicious food satisfies the body, so does song satisfy the soul. Music touches a place so deep and its effect is so profound as to be almost magical. Our minds have a special memory for music, perhaps due to the link with our inner being. A song can lift us as high as a prayer, music can bring us closer to God.

"THE HOARY HEAD IS A CROWN OF GLORY, IF IT BE FOUND IN THE WAY OF RIGHTEOUS."

PROVERBS 16:31

What values will you hold dear in your old age? What actions can you perform now, in order to be able to look back at your life when you are old and feel proud of what you have accomplished? Material possessions are important to acquire and work for, yet it is not what will make your legacy. Kindness, charity, happiness, and family values are some of the wondrous deeds that will leave an influence and impression on the world, your family, and friends. The details that bog us down in our daily life are not the important points to focus on or the problems that we will remember in our old age. Righteousness is attained, not acquired.

FISH

"REMEMBER THE DAYS OF OLD, CONSIDER THE YEARS OF MANY GENERATIONS."

DEUTERONOMY 32:7

Traditions are the living memory of those who came before us, as the traditions we create will be our link to future generations. Our present is informed by our past, by those whose wisdom endured and lives on through us. Recognize the beauty of our history and traditions, and the debt we owe to those who came before us. Celebrate your past—it has made you who you are.

Bursting with Flavor Tuna Patties

INGREDIENTS

2 cans tuna

1 egg

½ cup corn flakes crumbs

½ onion, chopped

1 clove garlic, minced

1 tablespoon soy sauce

½ tablespoon sugar

2 tablespoons ketchup

1 teaspoon sesame oil

½ teaspoon black pepper

¾ cup flour

3 cups oil, for frying

- Heat oil in a deep frying pan over medium heat.

- Mix all ingredients in a bowl.

- Form into small, round patties.

- Fry on both sides until golden brown.

CHEDDAR TILAPIA

Here in Israel, it is easy to find fresh produce. My neighbors all have goats and chickens and whenever we need fresh cheese or eggs we just walk over to their home and buy directly from them.

INGREDIENTS

8 tilapia fillets
1 cup cheddar cheese, shredded
¼ cup yogurt, plain and unsweetened
3 tablespoons mayonnaise
2 tablespoons lemon juice
Salt and pepper to taste
1 tablespoon canola oil

- Preheat oven to 400°F.

- Mix together all ingredients except the canola oil and tilapia fillets.

- Pour the oil into a medium-sized baking pan, and place the tilapia fillets on top of the oil.

- Bake for 10 minutes uncovered, then pour sauce over and continue baking until fish is cooked through (around 10 more minutes).

CREAMY CILANTRO SALMON

INGREDIENTS

6 1-inch wide pieces salmon fillet
½ cup mayonnaise
½ cup sour cream
3 teaspoons lemon juice
2 tablespoons fresh cilantro, chopped
Salt to taste

- Mix all ingredients together, except for fish.

- Spread some of the sauce over the salmon and then grill the salmon in a broiler for about 10 minutes.

- Pour the rest of the sauce on the salmon, then broil for another 2-3 minutes.

- Serve hot or cold.

MOROCCAN NILE

Israel is a melting pot of traditions and recipes from all over the world. This is a recipe that my 85-year-old Moroccan neighbor gave to me, and it has become one of my favorite fish recipes.

INGREDIENTS

5 Nile fish steaks (or perch)
3 tablespoons olive oil
¼ cup olive oil
½ cup water
2 tomatoes, diced
¾ cup lemon juice
1 red pepper, sliced
5 cloves garlic, chopped
4 tablespoons paprika
½ tablespoon cumin
Salt
1 bunch fresh cilantro

- Place 3 tablespoons olive oil, tomatoes, fish steaks, lemon juice, salt, sliced red pepper, and garlic in a big pot.

- Mix together ¼ cup olive oil, water, paprika, cumin, and salt. Pour over the food in the pot.

- Top off with fresh cilantro.

- Cook covered on medium heat for 50 minutes.

SALMON WITH SPINACH CREAM SAUCE

INGREDIENTS

6 1-inch wide pieces salmon fillet
2 cups frozen chopped spinach, thawed and drained
3 cloves garlic, crushed
½ cup sour cream
1 cup creamer
Salt and pepper to taste

- Preheat oven to 400°F.

- Place salmon in a medium-sized glass baking dish.

- Mix all ingredients together and pour over the salmon.

- Bake covered for 20 minutes. Baste the salmon in the sauce. Continue baking uncovered until salmon is cooked through (around another 10 minutes).

spice crusted salmon

SPICE CRUSTED SALMON

INGREDIENTS

6 2-inch wide pieces salmon fillet
Juice from one lemon
2 tablespoons olive oil
1 teaspoon sweet paprika
1 teaspoon garlic powder
½ teaspoon ginger powder
1 teaspoon dried dill
Salt and pepper to taste
1 cup Japanese bread crumbs (panko) or bread/corn flake crumbs

- Preheat the oven to 375°F.

- Place the salmon in a greased medium-sized baking dish.

- Cover the salmon in lemon juice and olive oil.

- Sprinkle all the seasonings over the salmon, and top with Japanese bread crumbs.

- Bake covered for 20 minutes, uncovered for 5 (until the salmon is cooked through).

TERIYAKI SALMON

This recipe is a traditional Eckstein recipe that my mother, my two sisters, and I all make regularly. Our kids all call it "Bubby's candy salmon," referring to my mother, who made up this delicious recipe. This salmon is the perfect mixture of sweet and salty!

INGREDIENTS

6 2-inch wide pieces salmon fillet
¼ cup soy sauce
¼ cup brown sugar
2 tablespoons water
¼ cup lemon juice
Salt to taste
¼ teaspoon ginger powder
1 tablespoon canola oil

- Preheat oven to 400°F.

- Mix together all ingredients, except the salmon, and pour the sauce over salmon in a medium-sized, greased baking dish.

- Let it marinate, if possible, for at least 30 minutes.

- Bake uncovered for 15 minutes (or until the salmon is cooked through). Baste the salmon every 10 minutes in the sauce.

If you'd like to grill the salmon instead: Pour the sauce over the salmon, let it marinate if possible, then grill for 20 minutes (or until the salmon is cooked through).

"HE BECOMETH POOR THAT DEALETH WITH A SLACK HAND: BUT THE HAND OF THE DILIGENT MAKETH RICH."

PROVERBS 10:4

We all have something special to give the world. Each individual has been provided by God with the unique qualities and abilities we need in this lifetime. What are your special gifts and how can you use them to help others? We all have the responsibility and the ability to engage in *tikkun olam*, repairing the world. What can you do today to make the world a better place? Our responsibility is to share what we have with others and in turn, others will share with us. Teachers, doctors, lawyers, rabbis, priests, and friends all share their strength to better the world. Become aware of your strengths, recognize, and appreciate them. Then, share your wisdom with others, and leave your heart open to learn from other people as well.

"MY FRUIT IS BETTER THAN GOLD, YEA, THAN FINE GOLD, AND MY REVENUE THAN CHOICE SILVER. I LEAD IN THE WAY OF RIGHTEOUSNESS IN THE MIDST OF THE PATHS OF JUDGEMENT."

PROVERBS 8:19-20

We learn from this verse that there is a connection between eating consciously and acting righteously. Try to appreciate where your food came from and give thanks for the energy that it provides you. Envision the fruits and vegetables starting off as little seeds, and the journey that they went through until they landed in your kitchen. When you look at the world through conscious eyes and are thankful for the little things that many people take for granted, it enables you to act in a righteous and just way.

SOUP

"I LOVE THEM THAT LOVE ME."
PROVERBS 8:17

If a person loves God, He loves them back. It is a very simple equation.
Love = love. Let us emulate God and give love freely to those who love
us and those who need us. If God can love us, surely we can love each
other.

CREAM OF CORN SOUP

INGREDIENTS

1 onion, chopped
2 cloves garlic, chopped
2 tablespoons canola oil
2 medium white potatoes, chopped
2 celery stalks, diced
2 tablespoons butter
7 cups water
¼ cup fresh parsley
1 tablespoon onion soup mix
1 (15-ounce) can corn
2 tablespoons cream cheese
Salt

- In a medium-sized pot, heat the oil.

- Add onion and garlic and mix over low flame until onion is cooked and clear.

- Add potatoes, celery, butter, and wait for the butter to melt.

- Cover the vegetables (except the corn) with water; bring to a boil.

- Add 1 tablespoon onion soup mix, fresh parsley, and salt.

- Simmer covered 20 minutes, then add corn.

- Blend everything together with an immersion blender.

- Add 2 tablespoons cream cheese and bring to a boil again.

CREAM OF ZUCCHINI SOUP

I always have zucchinis in my fridge, so when my children come home on a cold day and say that they want some hot soup, I'm always prepared for this recipe.

INGREDIENTS

1 onion, chopped
2 cloves garlic, chopped
2 tablespoons canola oil
2 medium white potatoes, chopped
3 zucchinis, diced
2 celery stalks, diced
2 tablespoons butter
7 cups water
1 tablespoon onion soup mix
¼ cup fresh parsley
½ teaspoon salt
2 tablespoons cream cheese

- In medium-sized or large pot, heat oil.

- Sauté onion and garlic until onion is cooked and clear.

- Add potatoes, zucchinis, celery, and butter, and wait for the butter to melt.

- Cover with water (around 7 cups); bring to a boil.

- Add onion soup mix, fresh parsley, and salt.

- Simmer covered 20 minutes.

- Blend everything together with immersion blender.

- Add 2 tablespoons cream cheese and bring to a boil again.

"WITHOLD NOT GOOD FROM THEM TO WHOM IT IS DUE."

PROVERBS 3:27

Actions or words that offend us or make us angry are often simply misunderstandings. When someone does or says something that hurts you, try to think about their intentions. Were they intentionally trying to cause you harm and pain? Were they personally going through a difficult time and simply took it out on you? Communication is the best path to healing, so tell the person how he or she hurt you – you might be surprised to find out that they weren't even aware of your injured feelings!

DELICIOUS ORANGE SOUP

INGREDIENTS

2 tablespoons canola oil
1 onion
2 zucchinis, chopped
3 sweet potatoes, sliced
3 carrots, chopped
½ squash, squared
1 white potato, sliced
1 tablespoon chicken soup mix
Salt and pepper to taste

- In a large pot, sauté onions and zucchini in heated oil until onions are clear.

- Add the rest of the vegetables and fill with water to cover around 3 inches above the vegetables.

- Turn the stove on high and add the spices.

- Once the soup is boiling, cover and lower the flame.

- Let the soup cook for around 30 minutes, or until all the vegetables are soft.

- Use a hand blender to blend the soup and make it creamy.

HEARTY VEGETABLE BARLEY

I used to go to restaurants to get vegetable barley soup until I realized how easy it is to make. This soup includes a variety of vegetables, and on cold winter nights, this soup makes a warm and comforting meal.

INGREDIENTS

1 onion, chopped
4 cloves garlic, chopped
2 tablespoons canola oil
10 cherry tomatoes, halved
1 yellow zucchini, sliced
1 green zucchini, sliced
2 carrots, chopped
1 sweet potato, sliced
2 celery stalks, chopped
½ cup cabbage (purple or white), chopped

¾ cup barley
12 cups water
4 tablespoons soy sauce
⅛ teaspoon black pepper
½ teaspoon dried parsley
1 teaspoon dried basil
¼ cup tomato paste

- Heat oil in large pot.

- Sauté onion and garlic until onion is cooked and clear.

- Add cherry tomatoes, yellow zucchini, green zucchini, carrot, sweet potato, celery, and cabbage. Sauté for 5 minutes.

- Add barley and 12 cups water; boil for 5 minutes.

- Simmer and add soy sauce, black pepper, dried parsley, dried basil, tomato paste, and salt.

- Simmer covered for 40 minutes.

Lentil, Split Pea, & Sweet Potato Soup

This soup is so filling that we often eat it for dinner. Easy and quick to prepare, this soup is always a hit with my family and guests. To give it an extra crunch, add soup nuts before serving.

INGREDIENTS

2 tablespoons canola oil
1 onion, chopped
4 cloves garlic, chopped
2 sweet potatoes, cubed
½ cup brown lentils
½ cup yellow split peas
½ cup green split peas
Water
1 tablespoon cumin
Salt and pepper

- Heat oil in medium-sized pot, and add onion and garlic.

- Sauté onion and garlic, until onion is clear and cooked.

- Add sweet potatoes, lentils, yellow split peas, and green split peas.

- Fill pot with water to 3 inches above the mixture.

- Boil for 45 minutes, adding more water as necessary.

- Add cumin, as well as salt and pepper to taste.

- Blend with hand blender (optional).

"HAPPY IS THE MAN WHO FINDETH WISDOM, THE MAN THAT GETTETH UNDERSTANDING."

PROVERBS 3:13

Much of the physical and emotional anguish that is rampant in our generation is caused by suppression of emotions. We are taught from a young age to swallow our feelings and put on a smile. Our natural instincts in regard to emotions have been lost. If we reclaim the understandings of our hearts, we will acquire wisdom and health. Think about the things that really make you sad and give those things legitimacy, no matter how petty or minute. Then, appreciate the happiness you feel from the small things. Perhaps it is a flower out your window that blooms, a delicious meal, a nice word from your spouse, a kiss from your child, a new pair of shoes. When you are aware of your own unique emotions and allow yourself to cry, laugh, or smile, then you will reclaim your own individual wisdom and completion. When you understand yourself you can understand the world around you.

TOMATO BISQUE

I have always enjoyed tomato bisque soup at restaurants, yet after trying many different recipes at home that weren't perfect, I decided to make my own recipe. Dozens of trials later, this is the tomato bisque recipe that my family and I like best, and it also happens to be quick and easy.

INGREDIENTS

2 tablespoons canola oil
30 cherry tomatoes, uncut, *or* 6 big tomatoes, diced
1 (15-ounce) can crushed tomatoes
2 onions
2 cups milk
1 (12-ounce) can coconut liquid *or* 2 cups dairy creamer
2 cups water
½ teaspoon salt

- In a medium-sized soup pot, heat oil.

- Sauté chopped onions and garlic in oil until onions are cooked and clear.

- Add cherry tomatoes (uncut) and a can of crushed tomatoes and let simmer for 5 minutes on a medium flame.

- Add milk, coconut milk *or* two cups of sweet dairy creamer, water, and salt; boil.

- Blend and serve!

MOMMA'S CAULIFLOWER SOUP

Just a few blocks away from my house in northern Israel are huge fields where farmers grow cauliflower, so my local community always has cauliflower in abundance. This creamy and savory soup takes just four ingredients and a few minutes to prepare.

INGREDIENTS

Water
1 head cauliflower, cut into pieces
1 medium to large Idaho potato, peeled and cubed
½ cup chicken soup mix
2 cups mozzarella or cheddar cheese, shredded

- Place cut cauliflower into a medium-sized pot, then fill the pot with water until it is almost to the top of the pot.

- Add potato and chicken soup mix.

- Bring to boil, cover, and simmer for 20 minutes.

- Using an immersion blender, blend potato and most of cauliflower, leaving some florets for garnish.

- Place a pinch of shredded cheddar or mozzarella cheese in each individual bowl immediately before serving.

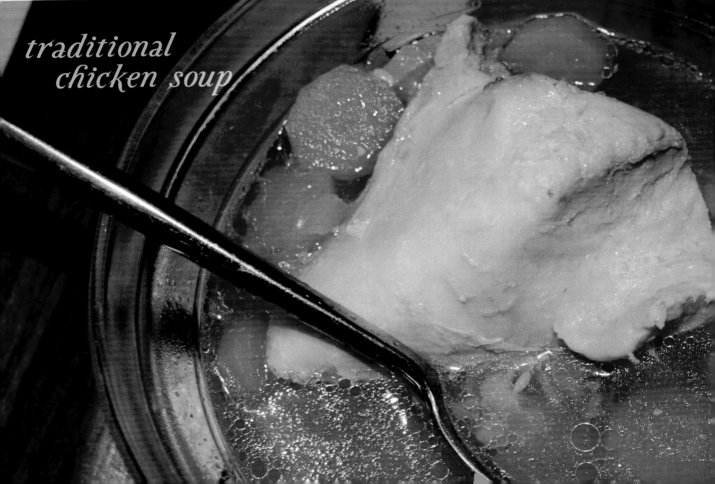

traditional chicken soup

TRADITIONAL CHICKEN SOUP

Chicken soup is a traditional dish in Jewish culture. Often on Friday nights when I was growing up, my mother would make this chicken soup. I feel blessed that today I get to pass on this tradition to my children!

INGREDIENTS

1 chicken, cut into 8 pieces
2 tablespoons canola oil
2 carrots, chopped
1 big onion, sliced
3 celery stalks, sliced
1 zucchini, chopped
1 tablespoon chicken soup mix
Salt and pepper
Fresh dill to taste

- In a large pot, heat oil.

- Add onions, celery, zucchini, and carrots; sauté for 5 minutes, stirring often.

- Add chicken and water to cover 3 inches above the chicken.

- Add chicken soup mix; salt and pepper to taste.

- Bring to boil and then simmer for 35 minutes, adding water as needed.

- Garnish with fresh dill.

"LET NOT MERCY AND TRUTH FORSAKE THEE: BIND THEM ABOUT THY NECK; WRITE THEM UPON THE TABLE OF THINE HEART."

PROVERBS 3:3

Mercy and truth are often challenged. We must bind them to us, inscribe them on our heart, make them a part of our very being. Imagine if all the world lived with truth and mercy. You can change the world.

"IF WE HAD TWO HEARTS LIKE
WE HAVE TWO ARMS AND TWO LEGS,
THEN ONE HEART COULD BE USED
FOR LOVE AND THE OTHER ONE FOR
HATE. SINCE I HAVE BUT ONE HEART,
THEN I DON'T HAVE THE LUXURY
OF HATING ANYONE."

—RABBI SHLOMO CARLEBACH—

NOTES

NOTES

NOTES

NOTES

NOTES

NOTES

NOTES